I WAS

The Stories of Animal Skulls

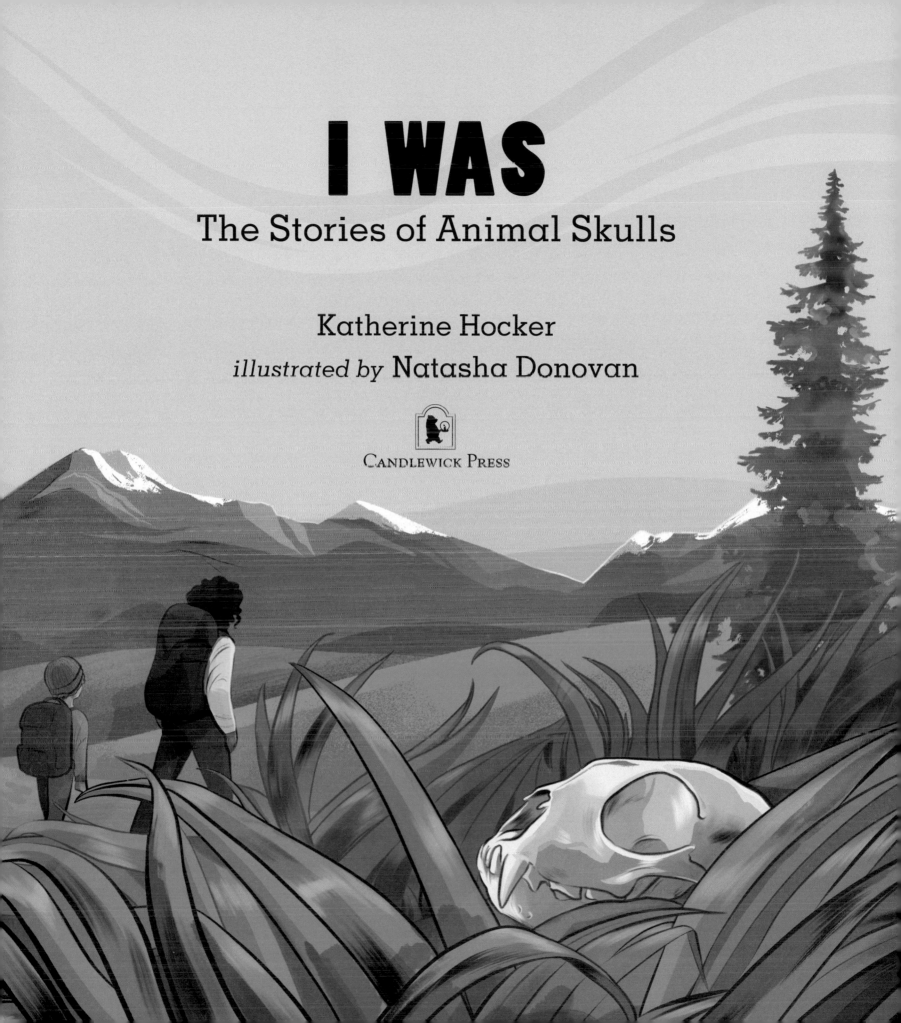

I WAS

The Stories of Animal Skulls

Katherine Hocker

illustrated by Natasha Donovan

CANDLEWICK PRESS

A SKULL SPEAKS in arches and ridges and caverns of bone.
It speaks in teeth and cracks, and holes into, and holes through.
It says:

I was.

See these hollows, wide as windows and round as moons?
They held my eyes.

I was the watcher in the winter forest.

When the light was so faint you called it darkness
and snowflakes wandered blind among the branches,
I hunted hares with my eyes full of light.

I was.

See this opening, filled with labyrinths of bone?
These bone scrolls formed my nose's warm chambers.

I was the one with my nose in the wind.

I smelled ripe apples and followed that scent down from the hillside and across the wide river, to the tree at the edge of your backyard.

I was.

Feel these teeth, cool and smooth, chisel-sharp?
They were my tools.

I was the tree cutter, the builder.

I tasted bark, then heartwood,
heard sticks snap as the tree fell.
I dragged branches one by one,
past your boot prints in the mud,
to the river bend where I built my dam.

I was.

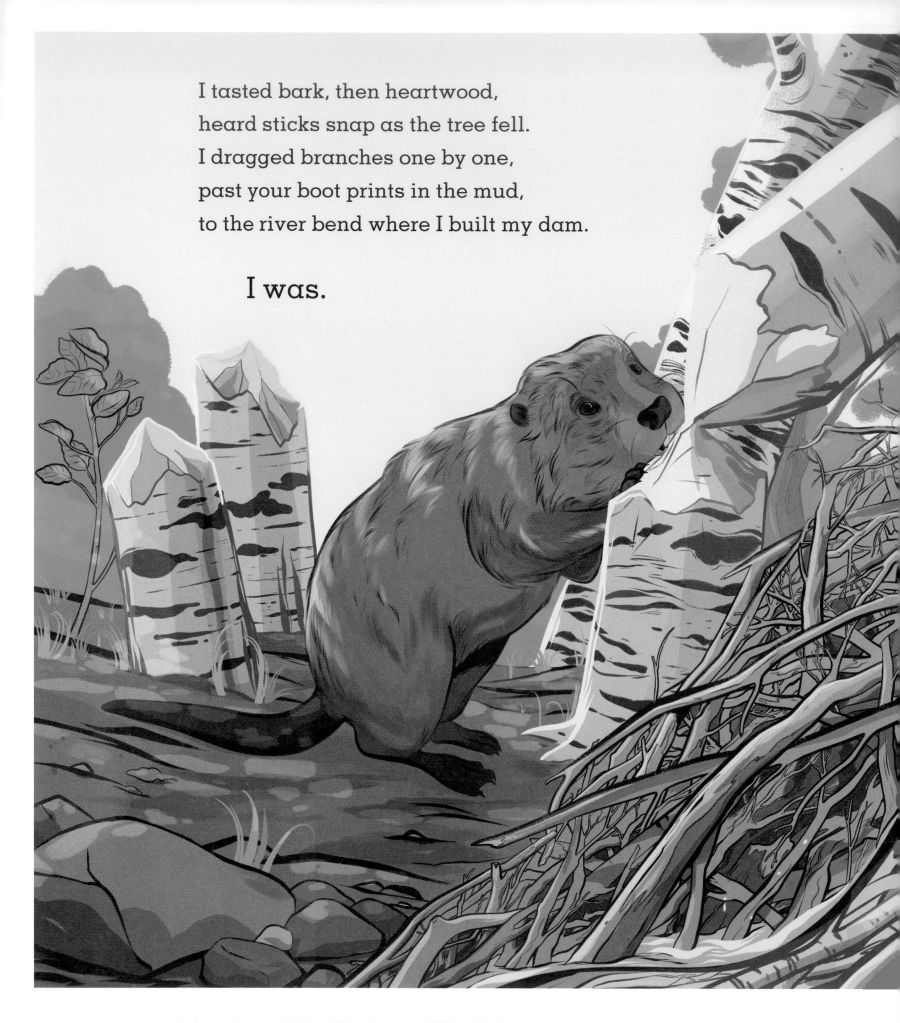

See this beak, slender and strong and sharp as a thorn?
It was my probe.

I was the seeker of sweetness.

I pushed my bill into a flower in your garden
and felt the pollen dust my forehead.
I drank the nectar of a thousand blossoms.

I was.

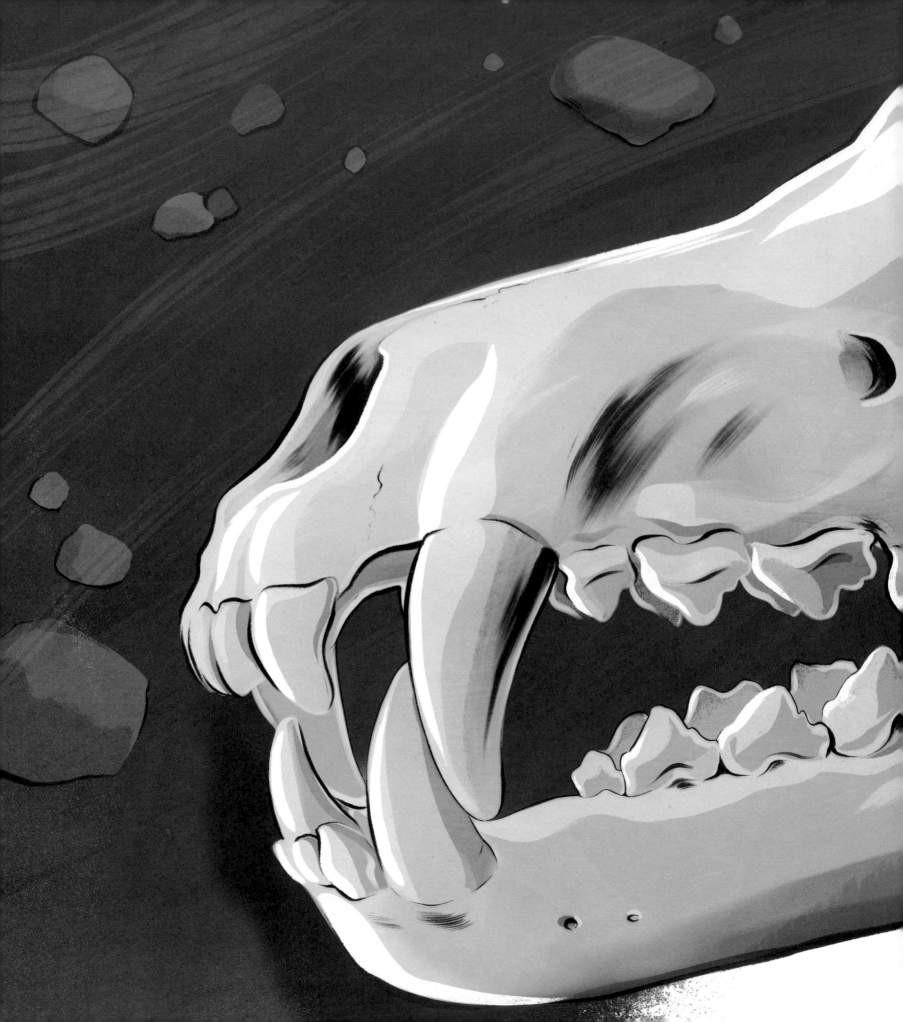

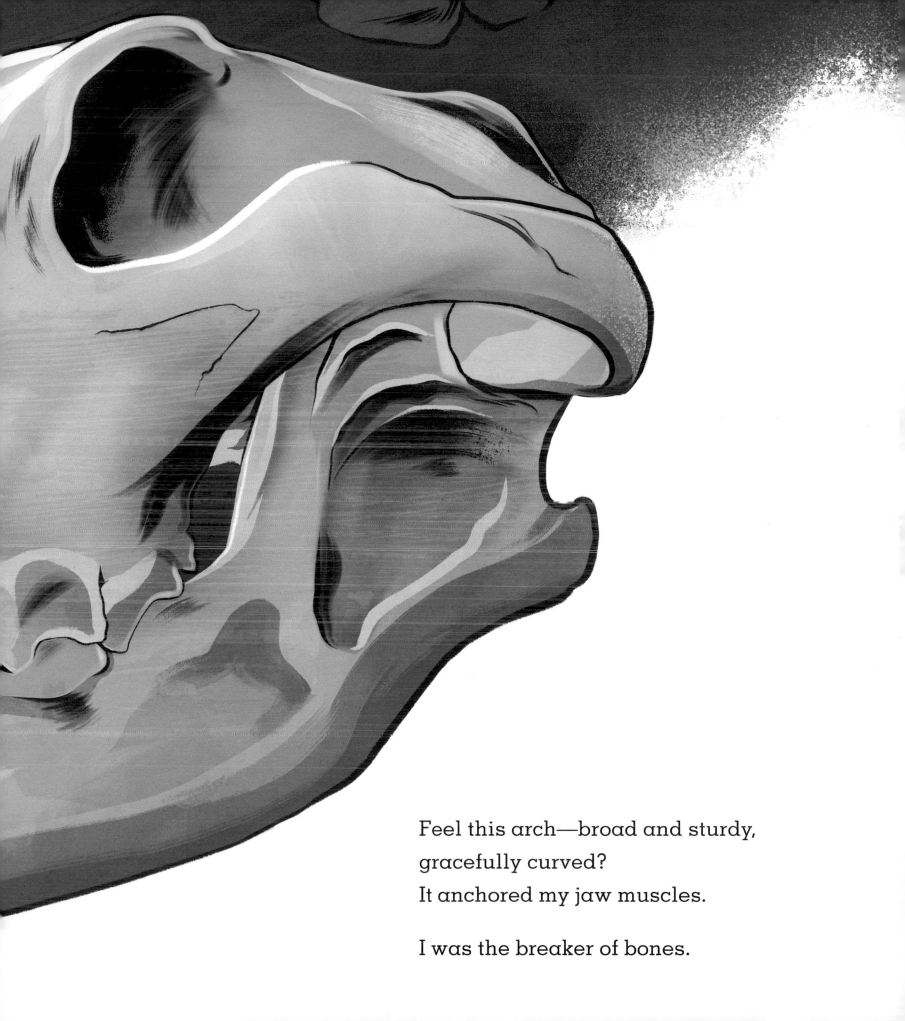

Feel this arch—broad and sturdy,
gracefully curved?
It anchored my jaw muscles.

I was the breaker of bones.

After the hunt was over,
after you heard my howls on the mountainside,
I cracked the big leg bones, lapped the rich marrow.

I was.

See these holes, curved and thin like open shells?
Those arches held my keen ears.

I was the listener in the night sky.

I heard you breathe as you admired my flight.
Among the whispers of the grass,
I found a mouse's heartbeat.
I dropped like an arrow, talons wide.

I was.

Your skull says: Feel this dome,
tall and wide and strong and smooth?

It shelters your mind.

You are the thinker—

you can calculate the paths of comets and stars.

You are the seeker—

you can learn your father's language, and your grandmother's too.

You are the wonderer—
you can listen to the stories of the skulls.

You are.

PARTS OF A SKULL

An animal's skull is a living sculpture of bone that protects its brain and cradles its eyes, ears, and nose. Each animal's skull has its own unique shape. Long after the rest of the animal is gone, a skull's shape can tell you about the animal's life.

Most skulls have the same basic parts:

The **cranium** is the upper part of the skull, including the eyes, ears, nose, and upper jaw. Every animal's cranium includes a strong chamber that held and protected its brain. This chamber is a reminder that—just like you—the animal had thoughts and memories, curiosity, intelligence, and consciousness.

The **mandible** is the movable lower jaw. The animal used it to eat, make noise, bite, and carry things.

The protective curves of bone that surround the eye sockets are called **orbits**. Their size and their position on the skull (front or sides, high or low) tell you how the animal saw the world.

Just like human-made tools, **teeth** are shaped for different jobs, so they can tell you how the animal gathered and ate its food. Instead of having teeth, a bird skull has a bony **beak**, which the bird used for eating, preening, and carrying things.

The inner chamber of the nose is called the **nasal cavity**. In most mammal and bird skulls, nasal cavities contain folds of delicate bone called **turbinates**. While the animal was alive, these bones were covered with living tissue that detected scent. The size of a skull's nasal cavity and the complexity of the bones inside it hint at the strength of the animal's sense of smell.

The openings where sounds enter the skull are called the **ear canals**. Located in the cranium behind the mandible, they lead to the inner ears, where sounds are detected. The position of the ear canals on a skull (high or low) can tell you about the animal's sense of hearing.

cranium

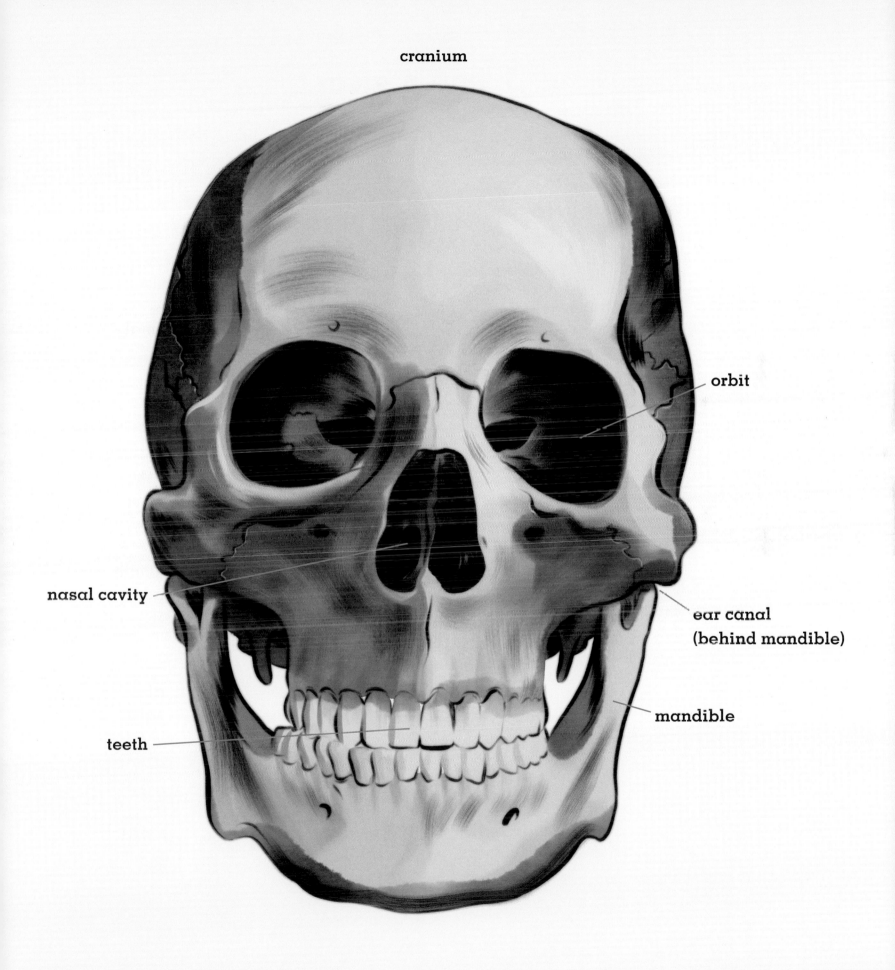

orbit

nasal cavity

ear canal
(behind mandible)

mandible

teeth

MORE STORIES

In this book, the skulls of lynx, deer, beaver, hummingbird, wolf, and owl each tell a story. Now that you've had a chance to learn about skull parts, take another look. What other stories do these skulls tell?

Lynx

- Forward-facing orbits allowed me to keep both my eyes on my prey, so I knew exactly how far to reach to grab it.
- My sharp side teeth slid along each other like scissors to slice through the skin and muscles of my prey.

Deer

- Sideways-facing orbits let me see danger coming from behind without having to turn my head.

Beaver

- My eyes and ear openings are at the top of my skull. If predators tried to attack me from above, I could see and hear them—and make a quick escape dive.
- My flat rear teeth mashed against each other, helping me grind my food of tough bark and stringy plants.

Hummingbird

- My skull bones are strong but paper-thin. Their lightness allowed me to fly.

Wolf

- I caught and killed large prey with my big, curved dagger-like fangs.
- My long nasal cavity, filled with complex turbinate bones, shaped my powerful sense of smell.

Owl

- I killed prey with piercing bites from my sharp, hooked beak.
- My huge eyes helped give me superb vision.

Your Skull

You can feel your own skull's strong and graceful shapes by gently touching your face and head. Feel the parts of your skull and compare them to the other skulls in this book. How are you like each animal? How are you different?

Below are some examples. What else can you find?

- Forward-facing orbits: Like the lynx and the owl, you can focus keenly on something in front of you. But unless you turn your head, you can't see behind you, as a deer can, or above your head, as a beaver can.
- Cutting teeth in the front of the jaw and grinding teeth at the back: Like the beaver, you can nip into hard foods such as celery with your front teeth and chew them thoroughly with your back teeth.
- Sharp, scissor-like teeth between the cutters and the grinders: Like the wolf and the lynx, you can slice through tough foods such as jerky with these side teeth.

LEARN MORE

To discover more skull stories, study lots of different animal skulls. Look for science books and websites with skull photos and information. You can see real animal skulls at some museums and nature centers. You might even find a skull yourself while exploring outdoors. If you do, observe it carefully: What stories does it tell?

Resources

Animal Skulls: A Guide to North American Species by Mark Elbroch. Mechanicsburg, PA: Stackpole Books, 2006.

Bones: An Inside Look at the Animal Kingdom by Jules Howard, illustrated by Chervelle Fryer. Somerville, MA: Candlewick Press, 2020.

"Skulls," California Academy of Science: https://www.calacademy.org/skulls.

To Mary Willson, my friend and fellow skull-seeker
KH

For the many nonhuman creatures of my life, both those who are no longer here and those who still are. You make each living moment so much richer.
ND

Text copyright © 2024 by Katherine Hocker
Illustrations copyright © 2024 by Natasha Donovan

First edition 2024

Library of Congress Catalog Card Number pending
ISBN 978-1-5362-2313-2

24 25 26 27 28 29 CCP 10 9 8 7 6 5 4 3 2 1

Printed in Shenzhen, Guangdong, China

This book was typeset in Memphis.
The illustrations were created digitally.

Candlewick Press
99 Dover Street
Somerville, Massachusetts 02144

www.candlewick.com